50 Nature Projects for Kids

STEP-BY-STEP

50 Nature Projects for Kids

Cecilia Fitzsimons

Photography by Anthony Pickhaver

SMITHMARK

For Steve and Caroline

This edition published in 1995 by
SMITHMARK Publishers Inc.
16 East 32nd Street
New York
NY 10016

SMITHMARK books are available for bulk purchase for sales
promotion and for premium use. For details write or call
the Manager of Special Sales, SMITHMARK Publishers Inc.
16 East 32nd Street, New York, NY, 10016; (212) 532–6600.

Produced by Anness Publishing Limited
1 Boundary Row
London SE1 8HP

ISBN 0 8317 7793 1

Publisher: Joanna Lorenz
Series Editor: Lindsay Porter
Designer: Peter Laws
Photographer: Anthony Pickhaver

CONTENTS

INTRODUCTION

The world of nature is all around us. Look out of the window and you will see birds, trees and plants. Some insects and spiders even come into our homes! But most of the time we hardly notice the living things that share our world.

It does not matter if you live in the city or in the countryside – this book will help you to open your eyes to nature. Learn to enjoy and help look after the natural world around us that we call the environment. There are plenty of fun things to do: nature projects, simple experiments, things to make and even games to play. This book is only a beginning, and once you start looking and observing, you will discover plenty of things for yourself.

Everytime you go outside, see how many different plants and animals you can see. The items on this tree stump were all found in a few minutes during a recent walk to our local woods. Conservation means looking after the environment and the animals and plants that live there. Try not to pick and take home any growing plants or living animals, and always ask permission before you borrow any materials, or go investigating out in nature.

NOTE

Many of the projects in this book are very easy and you will be able to do them by yourself. On some pages you will see this symbol:

!

This means that the activity may be dangerous and you must ask an adult to help you.

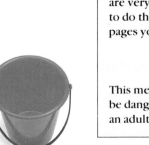

Materials and Equipment

Most of the materials and equipment you require for the projects will probably be found in your home. However, always ask someone before taking anything.

Bug box or lens
Use a bug box or lens to see the fascinating microscopic structure of many tiny creatures. Parts of plants such as leaves, seeds and petals can also be viewed in 'close-up'.

Camera and binoculars
These are expensive. They are not essential pieces of equipment, but are useful if you already have them, or can borrow them.

Field guides
These books will help you to identify the animals and plants that you can find. You can borrow them from your local library.

Gardening equipment
Gardening equipment such as bamboo canes, spades and trowels are always useful. They can be used in many nature activities and experiments.

Notebook and pencil
Record the things that you see with a notebook and pencil.

Paints, coloured pens and crayons
Use non-toxic paints and coloured pens to add colour to the drawings in your notebook.

Paper and card (cardboard)
A selection of different types of paper and card (cardboard) are useful for many activities and to display specimens.

Plastic bags
Collect and store specimens in plastic bags. They also stop seeds and young plants from drying out.

Plastic bottles
You can use plastic bottles over and over again. They are used to make several pieces of equipment.

Plastic buckets
Use a bucket to collect water and specimens in.

PVA (white) glue
This type of glue should be used in all projects in this book unless otherwise stated. Glue should be non-toxic and solvent free.

Scissors
Always take care when you use scissors. It is best to have an adult with you when using them. They should have rounded blades.

Sticky labels
Name your specimens on storage boxes and cards.

Sticky tape
Strong sticky tape is useful for making some of the projects.

String
String has many functions. It can be used to make equipment or for measuring things such as a tree trunk.

Supermarket packaging
Re-use plastic pots and boxes, plastic ice cream containers, jars, foam trays, burger boxes, foil dishes, etc. Use them for collecting, storage and making many pieces of equipment.

Tape measure or ruler
These are used to measure specimens and the length of materials you will need.

Torch (flashlight)
This is useful to shine into dark holes and corners and to study animals at night.

Tweezers and paintbrush
You need a steady hand to pick up tiny creatures. A pair of tweezers or a paintbrush will make the job easier.

Other materials used in this book are listed on each page.

bamboo canes

field guide

plastic bucket

notebooks

coloured pens

sticky labels

plastic bottles

plastic bags

paints

crayons

scissors

string

PVA (white) glue

paintbrushes

lens

tweezers

sticky tape

bug box

torch (flashlight)

paper

tape measure

supermarket packaging

camera

binoculars

Safety First

Here are a few important things to remember to protect yourself and the animals and plants in the countryside around you.

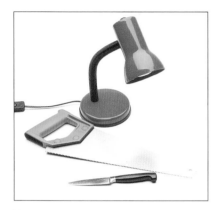

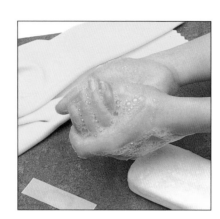

! **1** Sharp knives, tools and electricity are dangerous to use. Always ask an adult to help you with these.

! **2** Some animals can carry harmful germs. Always wash your hands after touching them. Germs also live in rivers and ponds. If you have cut your hand, put a plaster (band-aid) on it and wear rubber gloves before pond and river dipping. Always wash your hands afterwards.

! **3** Don't fall in! Be extremely careful near water, rivers, slippery rocks, sea, strong currents and soft mud. If it looks dangerous, do not go near it! Always ask an adult that you know and trust to come with you if you are out at night, or visiting wild and lonely places.

! **4** Some strong glue and paint can give off harmful fumes. Always use them in a well ventilated place, preferably outside. Always read the manufacturers' labels.

! **5** In some parts of the world there are dangerous animals and poisonous plants. Ask an adult if there are any animals or plants living nearby that may bite or sting.

! **6** Many fungi are poisonous. Do not touch any of them unless a qualified adult tells you that they are safe.

! **7** Many berries are also poisonous. Ask an adult to show you which ones are safe to eat or touch.

Country Code

Follow these simple rules for care and safety of the environment.

2 Return logs and rocks to the original position that you found them in. This will preserve the microhabitat (home) for the animals living underneath.

1 Don't pick wildflowers unless you have permission; it is illegal in many countries. Draw or photograph them instead.

4 Shut gates and keep to footpaths. Follow land-owners' instructions.

3 Keep your dog on a lead (leash) near farm animals.

!5 Be careful not to start fires. A dropped cigarette, broken glass or a barbeque can start a forest fire. Miles of habitat are destroyed and thousands of animals die in forest fires.

6 Take litter home. It looks ugly and can harm or kill many wild animals.

Collecting and Recording

The easiest way to study nature is simply to look and listen. But, if you write down the things that you see, you will remember them afterwards. Make a nature notebook or diary and you will soon see how things change throughout the year.

YOU WILL NEED
notebook
pencil
coloured pens

pencil

notebook

coloured pens

1 Every time you go out, you visit a habitat. This is the place where animals and plants live. It may be a park, a garden, a wood or by a lake.

2 In your notebook you should make a list and write about the different habitats that you have seen.

3 Each time that you go out, make a list of the different types of animals and plants that you see. Each type of animal or plant is called a species.

4 Certain animals and plants are often found together. These bees are feeding on knapweed. Write the following in your notebook: Where did you see the animals? What or who are they with? What are they doing?

5 Sometimes you will see something unusual, like this fairy mushroom ring. Write about it and draw or photograph it. Stick your photographs and postcards into your notebook later.

6 You may sometimes see an animal or bird that you do not recognize. Make a drawing of it in your notebook. Then you can identify it with a field guide when you get home. Make a note of different colours and patterns and write about where it was and what it was doing.

Nature Maps

Make a map of the area around your home. You can use it to work out a nature trail. Take your friends around the trail and surprise them with all the animals and plants that you can find.

YOU WILL NEED
notebook
pencil
coloured pens

pencil

notebook

coloured pens

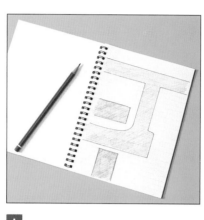

1 Draw a map of all the paths, roads, buildings and other man-made structures that you can see around your home. Colour them in grey or another suitable colour, such as brown.

2 Draw in the position of the grass, trees, hedges and other plants. Colour them in shades of green.

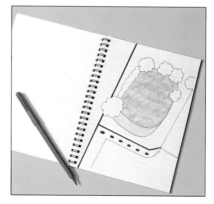

3 Draw in any puddles, ponds, rivers, rocks, logs, fences and any other special features that you can see.

4 On your map mark the position of any animals and plants that you find. Some may be walking around, so mark their path with a dotted line. You may only find clues, (footprints, droppings, etc) so mark these with a cross or a dot.

NATURE TIP
Use these notes and drawings to draw a large nature map of the area where you live.

In the Car

Car journeys can sometimes be long and boring. Help to pass the time by making a checklist in your notebook. You can check off all the natural things that you see along the way.

YOU WILL NEED
notebook
pencil
coloured pens

coloured pens

notebook

pencil

1 Make a list of the birds that you see along the way. Record how many of each you see.

2 Look for different flowers and trees on the side of the road. Look out for different colours of flowers and types of trees. Record how many of each you see.

3 Make a list of the animals you see. You can include farm animals. Record how many of each you see.

4 Make a list of the types of habitat that you pass on the way. Record how many of each you see.

Make Your Own Museum

As time goes by you will soon build up a large collection of natural bits and pieces.

Find somewhere safe to keep your collection of specimens, notes and pictures. You could store them in a box or a cupboard. If you can find a table that is not being used, you can create your own museum with a beautiful display as shown.

Specimens look good in clear plastic boxes or stuck onto card (cardboard). You can use double-sided sticky tape or strong PVA (white) glue to stick down feathers and other treasures that you find.

Look closely at the picture opposite. Many of the things that you can see have been made using the instructions in this book. Open the pages and start to collect objects for your own museum or nature table.

WOODS AND FORESTS

Parts of a Tree

Trees are the giants of the plant world. See if you can find these different parts of a tree.

2 Twigs: In winter, twigs and branches can help you to identify a tree. From the top, these twigs are: birch, ash, apple, oak and willow.

3 Trunk bark and roots: We do not often see a tree's roots. These willow trees are growing by a pond. Can you see the fine, hairy rootlets?

1 Leaves: These come in many shapes and sizes. Some have toothed edges. Others are divided up into many smaller leaflets. Pine leaves are like needles.

4 Flowers: Some trees have flowers with petals. But many have green or yellow catkins and do not look like flowers at all.

5 Fruit: There is a great variety of tree fruits and seeds. Fruit and nuts are spread by animals who try to eat them. Other seeds have wings that spin through the air like helicopters.

6 Cones: Pines are usually evergreen. Most do not lose their leaves in winter. Their leaves are like needles. Their fruit are seeds which are carried in pine cones.

7 Deciduous trees like the walnut opposite lose their leaves in winter. Every autumn the green leaves change colour to yellow, brown or red. They shrivel and fall from the tree. Can you see them on the ground?

How Tall is a Tree?

Field guides and other books often tell us the height of a tree. But how do we actually measure it?

YOU WILL NEED
pencil
stick
tape measure or ruler
notebook

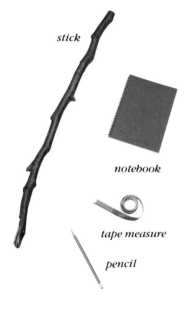

stick

notebook

tape measure

pencil

1 Stand in front of the tree. Hold out a pencil at arm's length so that you can see it and the tree at the same time. Ask a friend to stand at the bottom of the tree.

2 Line the pencil up so that the top of it is in line with the top of the tree. Move your thumb down the pencil until it is level with the bottom of the tree.

4 Mark the place where your friend is standing with a stick. Measure the distance from the stick to the tree. This distance is the same as the height of the tree. Record your findings in your notebook.

3 Turn the pencil so that it is horizontal, still keeping your thumb level with the bottom of the tree. Ask your friend to walk away from the trunk. Call and tell her to stop when she is level with the top of the pencil.

How Big and How Old is a Tree?

Some trees are very old. We can measure how big and old a tree is very easily.

YOU WILL NEED
rope
tape measure or ruler
notebook
pencil

notebook

rope

tape measure

pencil

1 How big is a tree? Take a piece of rope to measure the tree trunk. Put it around the tree and keep your finger on the place where the rope overlaps. A large oak tree like this one could be several hundred years old.

NATURE TIP

Next time you go for a walk look at the trees. How many really old trees can you find? These will be the tallest and/or those with the thickest trunks.

2 Lay the rope out straight on the ground and measure to the place you have marked with your finger. This will equal the distance around the outside of the trunk (the girth).

3 How old is a tree? The tree rings on a log can tell us its age. The tree grows a new ring every year.

4 Count the rings and you will discover the age of the log. If the tree has one hundred and fifty rings then the log is one hundred and fifty years old. Record your findings in your notebook with a pencil.

Growing a Tree

Trees are easy to grow at home. Collect some acorns, seeds or nuts in autumn and grow yourself a forest!

YOU WILL NEED
flowerpot
potting soil
acorn or other tree fruit such as nuts
   or seeds
plastic bag
rubber band
saucer
small trowel

flowerpot

potting soil

acorns

small trowel

plastic bag

rubber band

1 Fill the flowerpot with potting soil.

2 Push an acorn, nut or seed into the soil. Cover with more soil.

3 Water the flowerpot with just enough water to make the potting soil moist. Put the flowerpot into the plastic bag and seal the top with a rubber band. Leave on a windowsill until the acorn or seeds sprout. Be patient, this could take several weeks or even months.

4 Once the seeds have sprouted, remove the flowerpot from the plastic bag. Stand it in a saucer to catch any water that drains from the bottom. Keep the seedling on a windowsill and remember to water it regularly.

5 As your tree grows you will eventually need to repot it into a larger flowerpot.

6 When the young tree (or sapling) is 50–100 cm (18–39 in) tall, plant it outside in a place where it can grow into a large tree.

7 Look at the picture on the right. Can you see three stages in the life of an oak tree? The children are holding a seedling and a young sapling. Behind them is a young oak tree. Eventually this small tree will grow into an old giant of a tree – just like the one that was measured earlier.

Life in a Tree

Many animals make their homes among the leaves and branches of a tree. Beat a branch and discover the insects that live in the jungle world of the leaves.

YOU WILL NEED
large roll of white paper or cloth
stick
small paintbrush
collecting pots
lenses or bug box
field guide
notebook
pencil

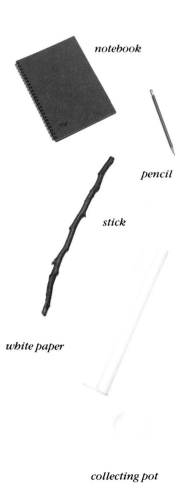

notebook

pencil

stick

white paper

collecting pot

1 Spread the paper or cloth under a large branch.

2 Shake the branch over the paper or cloth and beat it with a stick. Do not beat it too hard or you will crack the wood.

3 The insects will fall down onto the paper or cloth. Pick them up with the paintbrush and put them into the collecting pots.

4 Use lenses, a bug box, and a field guide to identify your specimens. In your notebook, write a list of everything that you have found. How many of each species are there? Make pencil drawings of them.

5 Release your captive insects, preferably under the tree that you found them in, or, at least somewhere safe. Now try beating a branch from a different type of tree. Which has the most insects living among its leaves?

Nature Detective

Whenever you are out near trees, look for clues to the animals that live there. Keep your eyes and ears open. Be a nature detective!

YOU WILL NEED
notebook
pencil
plastic bags
collecting box or pot

collecting box

plastic bags

pencil

notebook

1 Look for signs of feeding such as pine cones, nuts and fruit gnawed by squirrels, mice and other animals. Collect these specimens and record them in your notebook.

2 Look for nest holes. This hole goes down inside a hollow tree. It is being used by a fox. Look up into the branches of the tree and you may see woodpeckers' and other birds' nest holes.

3 Look for insect holes. Many insects and their larvae burrow into wood. These tunnels were made by bark beetles.

4 Look for rotten wood. Woodpeckers drill holes in rotten wood to look for burrowing insects. Other animals scratch at the wood to get at the insects inside.

Bark and Leaf Rubbing

Feel the ridges and veins on a leaf. By rubbing with a crayon you can use these ridges to make some beautiful copies of the leaves that you find.

YOU WILL NEED
paper
wax crayons or a soft pencil
folder
scrapbook
sticky tape or PVA (white) glue

folder

wax crayons

paper

1 For a bark rubbing, put a piece of paper against a tree trunk. Hold it firmly so that it does not move.

2 Rub the paper all over with a wax crayon or a soft pencil. The pattern of the bark will appear on the paper. Now try another tree. Different trees have different patterns of bark.

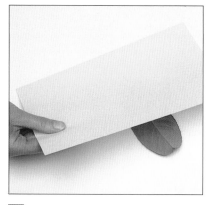

3 For a leaf rubbing, put a leaf on a smooth surface like a table. Cover with a piece of paper.

4 Hold the paper down firmly. Gently rub over the leaf with a wax crayon or soft pencil. You can store your finished rubbings in a folder or stick them into a scrapbook.

Collecting Spiders' Webs

Garden or orb-web spiders make beautiful webs that can be collected. This works best if you collect the webs on a wet, misty morning when they are covered with dew.

YOU WILL NEED
dark coloured card (cardboard) or paper
ozone-friendly hairspray
talcum powder
scissors

hairspray

talcum powder

dark coloured card (cardboard)

scissors

1 Find a web in a hedge, on a fence, or on a building. Choose one with enough space to easily slide a piece of card (cardboard) or paper behind it.

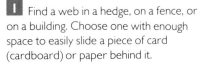

2 Spray the web with hairspray.

! SAFETY NOTE

Always make sure the web is empty before you take it. Some spiders can give a very nasty bite, or are even poisonous.

3 Shake talcum powder over the web. Then spray with hairspray again.

4 Slide the card or paper behind the web and lift it up so that the web is caught on the card. Cut the threads which attach the web. Leave the mounted webs to dry. If you do not smudge them they will stay like this for quite some time.

Who Lives Under Logs and Stones?

Many small creatures live in the soil and in the dark and damp places that they find under logs, rocks and stones.

YOU WILL NEED
paintbrush or tweezers
collecting box
notebook
pencil
field guide

collecting box

paintbrush

notebook

pencil

1 Find a brick, stone, rock, or a log to look under. You can also look under planks of wood and other garden rubbish.

2 Lift the object up gently to see if anything is living underneath. Gently pick up the creatures with a paintbrush or tweezers.

3 Put any animals that you find into the collecting box. Gently roll the log or rock back afterwards to stop the microhabitat underneath from drying out. Make notes, draw, and use a field guide to identify the animals you have found.

4 You may be lucky enough to find some larger animals such as frogs, toads or newts (salamanders). When you have made notes, take the animals back where you found them, and replace them gently.

NATURE TIP
It's fun to study small creatures, but remember always to take them back to their natural habitat.

A Pitfall Trap

A pitfall trap is used to catch small insects that walk across the top of the ground.

You will need
small trowel
small plastic collecting pot
4 stones
large flat stone
piece of wood or bark

small trowel

stones

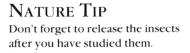

collecting pot

1 Dig a hole big enough for the plastic pot to sit in.

2 Put the pot in the hole and make sure the top is level with the ground. Fill in any holes around the edge.

3 Put four stones around the top.

4 Place a large flat stone and a piece of wood over the top so that it rests on the four smaller stones. Leave overnight. Next morning look to see if any bugs or other creatures have fallen into the trap.

Nature Tip
Don't forget to release the insects after you have studied them.

Tracks and Trails

Here are some clues to look for that animals have been near, even if you have not seen them.

1 Droppings: This has been left by an otter. It was found on a path by a river Can you see the fish bones and water beetle wing cases? These are all that remain from the otter's meal.

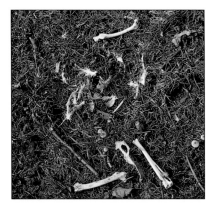

2 Signs of feeding: We can often see where an animal has been eating. These feathers and rabbit bones have been left by a fox.

3 Nests and burrows: These show us where animals live. Can you see the muddy path leading to this burrow?

4 Other signs: Many animals leave scratches and other signs behind them. This fur has been caught in a fence wire.

NATURE TIP

You can find tracks and trails everywhere. Sometimes they are found in unusual places. Look at the picture above. Can you see the snail trail leading up and down the wall of this house?

Watching Woodlice

Woodlice cannot live in dry conditions. This experiment shows how they actively seek damp places to live.

YOU WILL NEED
collecting box
2 sheets of paper towel
shallow plastic tray
newspaper

newspaper

collecting box

shallow plastic tray

paper towel

1 Look under stones, bricks and logs for some woodlice, and put them in the collecting box.

2 Fold one piece of paper towel in half and lay it down flat in one side of the tray.

3 Fold the second piece of paper towel in half, wet it and place it in the second half of the tray.

4 Pour the woodlice onto the middle of the tray and cover with newspaper. Leave for 30 minutes. Lift up the paper. Where have the woodlice gone?

Plaster Casts

Animals often leave their footprints in soft mud and sand. Make plaster casts of them to keep a permanent record. You can paint them when the plaster is dry.

YOU WILL NEED
strip of card (cardboard)
paperclip
plaster of Paris
water
bucket or plastic tub
spoon
small trowel
old brush or toothbrush (optional)

card (cardboard)

bucket

spoon

plaster of Paris

water

paperclips

1 Look for animal footprints in mud and sand.

2 Select the clearest footprint.

3 Put the card (cardboard) around the print and secure with a paperclip. Push the card down slightly into the mud.

4 Next, mix the plaster of Paris. Put a small amount of water into the bucket. Add plaster powder and stir well.

5 Pour the plaster into the mould and leave to set.

6 Once set, use a small trowel to dig up the plaster and print. Clean off the soil and sand. You may need to use an old brush or toothbrush to clean into all the small cracks.

Playing Conkers

Conkers is an old game played every autumn by children throughout the British Isles. It is named after William the Conquerer.

YOU WILL NEED
horse chestnuts, or sweet chestnuts if
    not available
skewer
string

skewer

string

horse chestnuts

1 Collect horse chestnuts that have fallen on the ground. Remove the nut from its case.

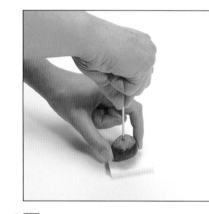

! 2 Ask an adult to help you drill a hole in the middle of the nut with a skewer.

3 Thread the string through the hole and tie a large knot in one end.

4 To play: The first player holds out their conker at arm's length. The second player hits the conker with theirs. Then you play in reverse. Repeat, taking turns, until one conker is broken.

! SAFETY TIP

Take care with this game! Do not eat horse chestnuts; they are mildly poisonous.

Making a Grass Squawker

This is a very simple reed instrument, but it is not very musical! It is a fun activity when out on a country walk.

YOU WILL NEED
blades of fresh grass
your hands

fresh grass

1 Look for some clean fresh grass. Carefully select and pick a long, wide blade of grass.

2 Put the blade of grass over one thumb, holding it in place with your forefinger.

NATURE TIP
Try different lengths and thicknesses of grass. Do they sound the same? If you make the hole between your thumbs bigger, does the sound change?

4 Blow through the little hole in between your two thumbs. It makes a horrible squawking noise! Replace the blade of grass if it splits.

3 Put your other thumb over the top so that the grass is held between them.

Autumn Harvest

Every year the autumn brings a rich harvest of fruit, vegetables, nuts and berries. This provides food for animals before the long winter months ahead. See if you can collect the types listed on this page.

YOU WILL NEED
basket or plastic bags
collecting pot
scissors, for snipping specimens

scissors

collecting pot

plastic bags

1 Berries that grow in hedges such as these elderberries and blackberries, have been used for centuries to make jams, fruit desserts and country wines.

2 There are different types of fruit. These fleshy fruits encourage animals to eat them and spread the seeds.

3 Nuts have a hard case to protect the seed within.

4 Seeds are produced in large numbers. They are also eaten by animals and birds.

5 These fruits are spread in the wind. Each has a tiny parachute of fine hairs or fluffy down.

6 Some fruits have hooks on them so that they catch onto animals' fur and our clothes. They can be carried for miles before they drop off and grow into a new plant.

Watching Animals at Night

Many animals visit our homes and gardens while we are asleep. Sometimes we are lucky enough to see them. If not, we can look for clues that they leave behind the next day.

YOU WILL NEED
torch (flashlight)
red tissue paper or cellophane
rubber band
lots of patience!

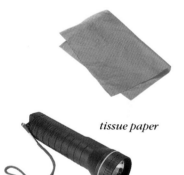

tissue paper

torch (flashlight)

rubber band

1 Cover a torch (flashlight) beam with red tissue paper or cellophane and hold it in place with a rubber band. You can shine this red light onto animals without frightening them.

2 At dusk look near trees, old buildings and lights for flying bats. Sometimes you can hear the high-pitched squeaks and clicks that they make when hunting for moths and other flying insects.

3 Look for clues such as droppings, signs of feeding, garden damage and spilt dustbins (garbage cans). (Racoons and foxes often knock these over.)

! 4 You can put food out as bait to attract wild animals and birds into your garden but you must get permission from an adult first. Try cat food, bread, grain, peanuts and peanut butter.

Making a Hide

A hide makes you invisible. You can watch animals without frightening them. Build one near a bird table and watch the birds come to feed.

YOU WILL NEED
4 long and 4 short bamboo canes
string
scissors
large dark cloth
large safety pins

bamboo canes

cloth

scissors

string

1 Put four long canes into the ground.

2 Tie the remaining shorter canes in a square around the top.

NATURE TIP

Take a notebook and pencil into the hide so you can record what you see. Look in a field guide afterwards to identify anything you don't recognize.

3 Cover with the cloth.

4 Use safety pins to join the sides, but leave spaces big enough to look through. Remember to be very still and quiet or you will frighten away the animals you are trying to watch.

Keeping Slugs and Snails

Slugs and snails can be kept in a tank. Here, you can learn how to make them a comfortable home.

YOU WILL NEED
gravel
small tank or large plastic
  ice cream container
soil
moss and grass
small stones, pieces of bark and
  dried leaves
gauze or netting
string
scissors

small tank

gauze

string

soil

gravel

moss

stone, bark and dried leaves

1 Put a layer of gravel in the bottom of the tank or container.

2 Cover the gravel with a layer of soil.

NATURE TIP

Keep your snails in a cool place. Feed them on a small amount of breakfast cereal (not too sugary), and small pieces of fruit and vegetables. Add fresh grass and leaves when needed.

3 Plant pieces of moss and grass in the soil. Add stones, bark and the dried leaves. Water the tank just enough to moisten the soil.

4 Put in a few slugs or snails and cover the tank with a piece of gauze or netting. Tie it down with string or replace the lid. Make sure that it has plenty of air holes.

Tracking Snails

Garden snails sleep together in a big cluster called a rookery. They often return to the same place to sleep day after day.

YOU WILL NEED
child's peel-off nail polish
flowerpot
small stone

stone

flowerpot

nail polish

1 Search in a garden or park for a group of sleeping snails.

2 You will find them clustered together under logs, rocks or bricks.

3 Pick out 10 snails. Put a small dot of nail polish on each of their shells.

4 Collect your marked snails. Put them under an upturned flowerpot nearby. Put a stone under the rim of the flowerpot so that the snails can crawl out. The next morning, see if you can find the snails. Are they still under the flowerpot?

NATURE TIP
After you have found the snails, gently peel off the nail polish, otherwise the bright colour will attract the birds.

Keeping Earthworms

Earthworms are good for the soil. As they dig their burrows they mix up the soil. They also pull leaves down from the surface. This helps to fertilize the soil.

YOU WILL NEED
plastic bottle
scissors
gravel
soil
funnel (optional)
sand
dried leaves
plastic pot the same width as the bottle
black plastic bag (optional)

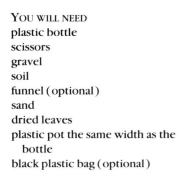

plastic pot

black plastic bag

gravel

soil

funnel

plastic bottle

sand

dried leaves

scissors

1 Cut the top off the bottle.

2 Put a layer of gravel in the bottom of the bottle.

3 Put a layer of soil on top. (You may need to use a funnel to do this.)

4 Put a layer of sand on top. (You may need to use a funnel to do this.)

5 Repeat the soil and sand layers until you have filled the bottle almost to the top. Add just enough water to moisten the soil layers, but not too much or your worms will drown.

NATURE TIP

Worms do not like bright light so keep the bottle in a cupboard or cover with a black plastic bag. Give your worms more leaves when they need them. What happens to the layers of soil?

6 Put some worms on top of the soil and cover with dead leaves. Make holes in the bottom of a plastic pot. Turn it upside down and use it to cover the top of the bottle, like a lid.

Making a Keep Net

This keep net is a safe way to watch butterflies for a short time without hurting them.

YOU WILL NEED
netting or gauze
scissors
needle and thread
4 bamboo canes
butterfly or fishing net
notebook
pencil

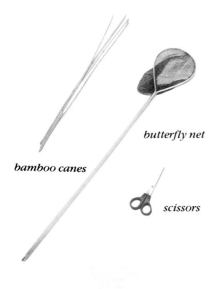

butterfly net

bamboo canes

 scissors

netting

NATURE TIP
Butterflies drink sugary nectar from flowers. Plant these flowers in your garden and the butterflies will come to feed from them: buddleia, lavender, golden rod, iceplant, hyssop, asclepias (milkweed) and honeysuckle. Cabbages, nasturtiums and stinging nettles also attract butterflies. They lay their eggs on these plants.

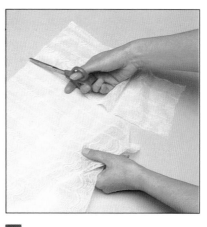

1 Cut a square piece of netting 30 cm × 30 cm (12 in × 12 in) and a rectangle of netting 120 cm × 50 cm (48 in × 20 in).

2 Fold the rectangle in half. Sew the long sides together.

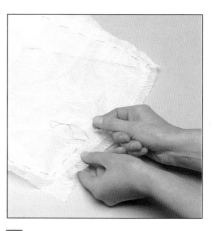

3 Sew the square top onto one end.

4 Push four garden canes into the ground in a square, each 30 cm (12 in) apart. Drape the net over the top.

5 Carefully catch a butterfly with a butterfly or fishing net and gently put it into the net. Try not to touch the butterflies' wings or you could injure them.

6 Look through the net to identify your butterfly. This one is a small tortoiseshell. Draw it and make notes in your notebook. Release the butterfly afterwards.

Keeping Caterpillars

This is a nice clean way to keep caterpillars.
Eventually they will turn into pupae and then
into beautiful butterflies and moths.

YOU WILL NEED
collecting pot
plastic bottle
scissors
paper towels
large jar
sticky tape
gauze or netting
rubber band or string

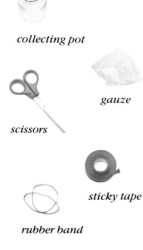

plastic bottle

collecting pot

scissors

gauze

sticky tape

rubber band

1 Look for some caterpillars living on cabbages and other plants. Put them in a collecting pot. At the same time, collect some leaves from the plants that you found the caterpillars living on.

2 Cut the bottom from the plastic bottle with a pair of scissors.

3 Take a bunch of leaves and foliage that you found the caterpillars on. Wrap a piece of paper towel around the stalks of the leaves.

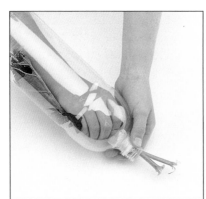

4 Put the leaves inside the bottle and push the stalks through the neck so that the tissue forms a plug.

5 Stand the bottle neck-down in a jar of water. Make sure that the plant stalks are standing in the water. Tape the bottle to the jar if it is wobbly and does not stand firmly.

NATURE TIP

Every few days, clean out the bottle, wash it, dry it, and give the caterpillars fresh plants to eat. Eventually the caterpillars will pupate. They will turn into sausage-shaped pupae. You can keep them until the butterflies or moths emerge, and then you must release them outside.

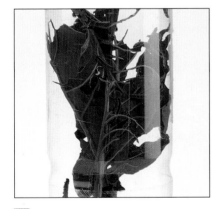

6 Put the caterpillars inside the bottle. Cover the top with a piece of gauze. Hold it in place with a rubber band or tie with string. Feed your caterpillars regularly.

Growing Wildflowers

Wildflowers are easy to grow from seed and can be very attractive in your garden. They will encourage more insects to visit them, who will in turn attract more birds to your garden.

YOU WILL NEED
seed tray or flowerpot
soil
packet of wildflower seeds
plastic bag

seed tray

soil

plastic bag

1 Fill the seed tray or flowerpot with a layer of soil.

2 Sprinkle on the seeds.

3 Cover the seeds with a layer of soil.

4 Water, and then cover the seed tray or pot with a plastic bag. Leave on a windowsill

5 When the seedlings have sprouted, remove the plastic bag. Water regularly. As they grow larger, plant the seedlings into larger flowerpots or directly into your garden.

Bird Table (Feeder)

Wild birds need feeding, especially in winter time when there is little food available. Some people think you should not feed birds in spring, because chicks can choke on foods like peanuts. It is probably better not to put out any peanuts at this time of year. You will need an adult's help for this project.

YOU WILL NEED
4 strips of wood, 27 cm (10¾ in) long
square piece of wood, 30 cm × 30 cm
  (12 in × 12 in) and approximately
  1 cm (½ in) thick
nails
hammer
varnish
paintbrush
screw-eyes
string (optional)

hammer

wood

nails   *screw-eyes*

string

1 Nail the thin strips of wood around the edges of the square piece. Leave a gap at each corner to allow the rain water to drain away.

2 Varnish and leave to dry. Screw a few screw-eyes to the underneath of the board. You can hang food from these afterwards.

3 Fix to the top of a tall post by hammering two or three nails through the middle of the board and into the post below.

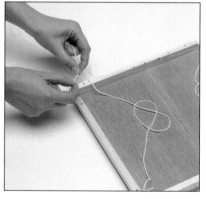

4 Alternatively, screw in one screw-eye to each corner on the upper surface. Tie on two loops of string by knotting the ends through the screw-eyes. Then you can hang the table (feeder) from a suitable tree or hook. A hanging table is best if cats are a problem in your garden

Feeding Winter Birds

Choose some of these ideas to feed birds in winter.

YOU WILL NEED
Choose food from the following:
dried bird food
dried seed heads such as corn cobs,
   millet and sunflower
peanuts
bread and cake crumbs
coconut
lard or other hard fat
chopped bacon rind

bowl of water
peanut feeder
string
scissors
spoon
supermarket packaging such as plastic
   pots or nets

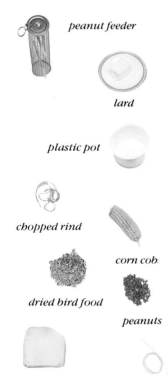

peanut feeder

lard

plastic pot

chopped rind

corn cob

dried bird food

peanuts

bread

string

1 Dried food is the easiest to put out. Give the birds grain, sunflower seeds, peanuts (but not in spring), bread and cake crumbs. Do not forget to also give them a bowl of water to drink.

2 Hanging food allows birds to perch on the food. Hang strings of peanuts, half a coconut, a dried sweet corn cob, millet or other seed heads from the screw-eyes on your bird feeder. You can also hang these foods from the branches of nearby trees. Put loose peanuts in a peanut feeder, if feeding in the winter.

3 Birdy cake is a rich food for cold winter weather. Soften lard or a similar hard fat in a warm place. Mash in mixed grains, crumbs, bread, chopped bacon and rinds. Mix well.

4 Press into supermarket packaging such as plastic pots and nets. Set until hard in a refrigerator. When set, tip the birdy cake from the pots and put on the bird feeder or hang the nets beneath it.

Making a Nesting Box

This box will attract small birds to nest in your garden. Once they have taken up residence, the birds will return year after year.

YOU WILL NEED
pencil
ruler
piece of wood, 147 cm × 15 cm × 1 cm (58 in × 6 in × ½ in)
saw
drill with 3 cm (1¼ in) drill bit
nails
hammer
hinge
screws
screwdriver
varnish
paintbrush

varnish

hinge

nails

hammer

drill bit

saw

ruler

pencil

1 Use a pencil and ruler to mark out the wood. Follow the diagram opposite.

! 2 Ask an adult to help you to cut the wood.

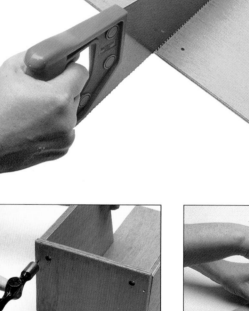

! 3 Ask an adult to drill a large hole 3 cm (1¼ in) in diameter in the front of the box. Drill four small holes in the bottom of the box and two in the back.

4 Nail the sides together and nail on the bottom of the box.

5 Screw a hinge onto the lid and attach it to the box.

6 Varnish the box and allow to dry Place high up on a tree, post or garden shed. Attach by hammering a nail through the two holes in the back.

Making a Light Trap for Moths

Moths and other insects fly at night. They are attracted to the bright lights of electric lightbulbs. You can study them using this simple piece of equipment.

YOU WILL NEED
large, thick plastic bottle (the type used for household cleaning liquids)
scissors
sticky tape
desk lamp
small collecting pots
paintbrush
field guide
notebook
pencil

plastic bottle

desk lamp

collecting pot

scissors

sticky tape

paintbrush

! **1** Ask an adult to clean the bottle, and cut the top off to make a funnel.

2 Stand the top upside down in the base of the bottle. Tape the two together.

3 Take the light trap outside. Place a desk lamp so that it shines over the top of the funnel. You may need to stand the lamp on a brick if it is too short.

! **4** Ask an adult to plug the lamp into the nearest electricity socket. DO NOT USE IN WET WEATHER. At night, turn the lamp on and leave the light shining for several hours.

5 Moths fly into the light and fall down into the funnel. They are then trapped in the bottom section. Remove the funnel and see which moths and other flying insects have been caught in the bottom of the bottle.

6 Put the moths and insects into small collecting pots, using a small paintbrush to pick them up gently. Identify them with a field guide, and make notes and drawings about them in your nature notebook. Carefully release the moths and insects afterwards.

Making a Plankton Net

This net is used to catch tiny water creatures that
would pass through the holes in a normal fishing net.

YOU WILL NEED
thick wire
old pair of tights
scissors
long bamboo cane
string
small plastic jar

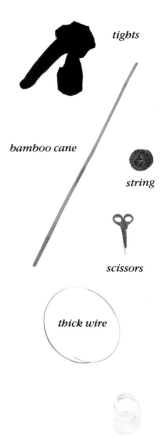

tights

bamboo cane

string

scissors

thick wire

plastic jar

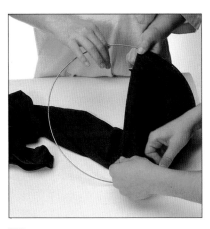

1 Thread the wire through the waist of the tights.

2 Cut the legs off the tights.

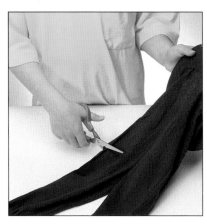

3 Twist the ends of the wire together.

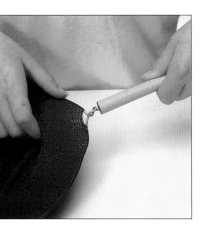

4 Push the twisted wires into the end of the cane.

5 Use string to tie the bottom of the net around the neck of the jar. Tie as tightly as you can.

6 When you use this net the pond animals are caught in the jar at the bottom.

Pond and River Dipping

Beneath the surface of the water lives a rich and varied animal and plant life. Dip into the world of a pond or river using a fishing or plankton net and discover the creatures that live there.

YOU WILL NEED
ice cream container or bucket
fishing and/or plankton net
shallow white dishes, made by cutting
   the top from an ice cream container
paintbrush
jam jar or tank
notebook
pencil

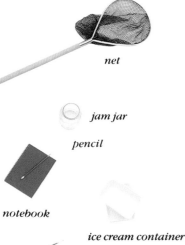

net

jam jar

pencil

notebook

ice cream container

paintbrush

1 Fill an ice cream container or bucket with pond water. You will then have something to put your animals in as soon as you catch them.

2 Sweep the fishing or plankton net through the weeds.

3 Pour the water from the plankton net into an ice cream container or bucket by pushing the jar up through the net. Pull the net back and pour the water out.

4 You will soon catch many different animals. Here are two types of pond snail – a round Ramshorn Snail and a pointed Greater Pond Snail.

5 Carefully pick out the animals you have just caught with a paintbrush and place them into a clean shallow dish or ice cream container, of water. You will have caught a lot of rubbish such as dead leaves, and the clean water will help you see the animals more clearly.

SAFETY TIP
Take care around water, no matter
how shallow it seems.

6 You can also put them into a large
jam jar, or small tank. Identify the species
you have found and make notes in your
notebook. Visit different ponds, lakes, and
rivers. Do you find the same species living
in different places?

Making a Freshwater Aquarium

Pond animals can be kept easily in an aquarium. Watch the busy lives of your pond animals.

YOU WILL NEED
aquarium gravel
bucket
large tank
newspaper
waterplants
stones or rocks
seashells (optional)
fish or other creatures collected from
    a pond or river

rock

aquarium gravel

newspaper

tank

1 Wash the gravel in a bucket. Keep stirring it under running water. You must do this thoroughly to remove dirt from the stones which will make the water in your tank cloudy.

2 Put the gravel in the bottom of the tank. Once you have filled the tank with water it will be too heavy to move – so decide where you want to keep it now. Do not place the tank in bright sunshine or the water will get too hot and your animals will die.

3 Put the newspaper over the top of the gravel. Slowly pour the water on to of the paper. This prevents the water from becoming too cloudy.

4 The water will be slightly cloudy, so leave the tank to clear for several days.

5 Add some waterplants and the rocks. Put the roots of the plants under the rocks to stop them from floating up to the surface. If you use any seashells, make sure that they have been well washed in fresh water to remove any salt that they may contain.

6 Put in the animals that you have collected from a pond or river. If you are going to have fish in the aquarium, only choose small ones or else they will eat all of your pond animals.

Building a Pond

Build a pond and attract more wildlife into your garden. You will be surprised just how quickly insects and other creatures will move in to use it.

YOU WILL NEED
string (optional)
spade
newspapers, old carpet, or sand
sheet of plastic or rubber pond liner
soil, logs or slabs
waterplants
fish or other creatures collected from
    a pond
home-grown wild flowers

spade

newspapers

sheet of plastic

! 1 With an adult's help, mark out the shape of the pond that you would like with string – or just mark a line in the grass. Cut the turf with a spade.

! 2 Dig a hole for the pond. Try to make several levels. Remove any large stones from the bottom.

3 Line the hole with newspapers, old carpet or sand.

4 Cover with a sheet of plastic or a pond liner. Carefully mould the liner to the shape of the pond. Do not stand in the pond because you will make a hole in the liner.

5 Put soil, logs or slabs over the edge of the liner. Make sure that the edge of the liner is completely covered all the way around. Fill the pond with water and leave to clear.

6 Add waterplants which are growing in pots and stand them on a brick if the water is too deep. Add fish and pond animals. Plant wildflowers that you have grown around the edge of the pond. Leave nature to do its work and in a few months you will have a mature and well established pond.

Making a Fishing Net

This net is a useful piece of equipment which is easy to make. Use it to catch flying insects, or for pond dipping and rock pooling.

YOU WILL NEED
rectangle of netting, 90 cm × 30 cm
   (36 in × 12 in)
needle and thread
wire coathanger
scissors or pliers
bamboo cane
jubilee clip or wire

netting

bamboo cane

pliers

wire coathanger

jubilee clip

thread

scissors

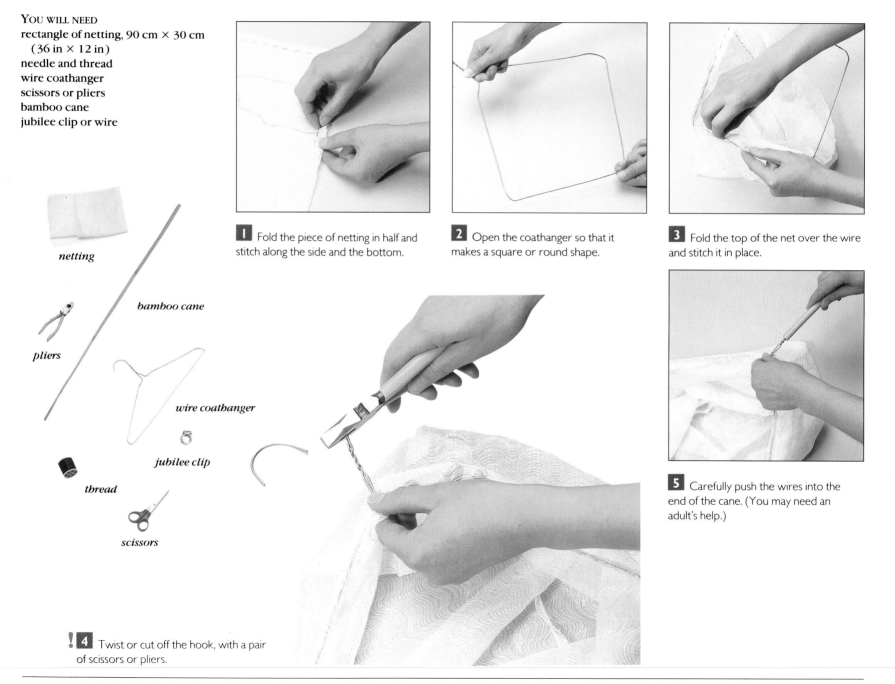

1 Fold the piece of netting in half and stitch along the side and the bottom.

2 Open the coathanger so that it makes a square or round shape.

3 Fold the top of the net over the wire and stitch it in place.

5 Carefully push the wires into the end of the cane. (You may need an adult's help.)

! 4 Twist or cut off the hook, with a pair of scissors or pliers.

6 Secure the net to the cane with a jubilee clip or a piece of wire tightly twisted around the top. This will stop the net falling off if you get it caught up in pond weeds.

Beachcombing at the Seaside

We all like to go to the seaside. Be a nature detective on the beach and see what treasures you can find.

YOU WILL NEED
bucket
plastic bags
notebook
pencil

pencil

notebook

plastic bags

bucket

1 Look for animals under seaweed and rocks where they stay nice and damp. Cuttlefish, crab and urchin shells, feathers and other animals are often washed up. You will find them at the highest place reached by the tide, known as the strandline.

2 You will find a variety of shells all over the beach.

3 Look for unusual stones and pebble sculptures, fossils and minerals. The holes in this large stone were drilled by rock-boring clams. Can you see the Indian's head? This is a real stone that was just picked up on a beach.

4 Who lives under the sand? Look for worm holes and dig down to find the worm beneath. Collect animals and shells and put them in a bucket or plastic bags. Make notes in your notebook, and release living creatures afterwards.

! 5 A lot of garbage is washed up onto the beach. Ropes, plastic and driftwood are harmless, but fishing tackle, bottles and canisters can be dangerous. Take care and do not touch. Some can contain dangerous chemicals.

Beach Transect

Many creatures make their home on the beach, but we have to search hard to find them. The sea comes up and down the beach with the tides, so different animals and plants are found at different levels of the beach – from the top to the bottom, nearest to the sea. A transect is a way of measuring these changes.

YOU WILL NEED
long roll of string
bamboo canes
notebook
pencil

pencil

notebook

bamboo canes

string

I Take a long piece of string and stretch it from the top of the beach towards the sea. Use bamboo canes to hold the string up. Starting from the top of the beach, walk along the string towards the sea. Every 50 paces, stop and write down all the animals and plants that you can find at each place in your nature notebook.

!SAFETY TIP
Take care on slippery rocks. Do not
get cut off by incoming tides.

2 At the top of the beach (as close to the land as possible), you will find a few types of land plants that can live in these salty places.

3 The strandline (high tide line) is the highest place reached by the high tide. Sandhoppers and seaweed flies live here.

4 On the upper shore you will find green seaweed.

5 The middle shore is often covered by wide banks of brown seaweed called wrack (rockweed) and by barnacles covering the rocks.

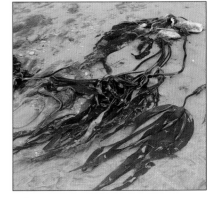

6 You are on the lower shore when you find red seaweed and large brown seaweed called kelp attached to rocks. This part of the shore is only exposed at low tide and is where you will find most animals living.

Rock Pools

Many animals such as shrimps, crabs and baby fish live in rock pools. Here they find a safe place to wait until the tide comes in again.

You will need
fishing net
bucket
plastic bags
notebook
pencil

fishing net

bucket

pencil

notebook

plastic bags

1 When the tide goes out, animals on the beach must close up or hide and wait until the water returns. In the rock pool however, the animals can continue to swim and feed.

2 Some animals such as limpets and anemones attach themselves to rocks. They can move, but only very slowly.

3 Sweep a fishing net through the sandy bottom of the pool. You may catch shrimps, crabs and tiny fish that lie buried in the sand.

! 4 Be careful if you find a crab. Do not handle it roughly because you may damage its legs. You can pick it up safely by holding it across the back of its shell. This way it cannot nip you!

5 Lift up rocks carefully. Many animals live underneath them. Always replace rocks gently so that you do not damage the microhabitat and the animals underneath.

6 Collect animals in a bucket or plastic bag. Identify them and make notes in your notebook. In this bucket there are hermit crabs, shore crabs, periwinkles and a sea anemone. Do not forget to release them into the water afterwards.

! Safety Tip
Take care on slippery rocks. Do not get cut off by incoming tides.

Beach Art

You can never get bored on a beach. Draw pictures in the sand or create these masterpieces.

1 Collect shells on the beach and arrange them to make a picture.

2 Decorate your picture with seaweed, stones, feathers and driftwood – in fact anything that you can find.

5 This face is made from seaweed and stones.

NATURE TIP

You could take a picture of your beach art so you can remember it after it has been washed away.

3 This driftwood ship has a stone cabin and funnel. The smoke and sea are made of seaweed. The sand below is rippled and looks like waves.

4 Different shaped seaweeds look like trees and plants in a garden.

Seaweed Pictures

Making seaweed pictures was a popular pastime during Victorian times, 100 years ago.

YOU WILL NEED
shallow dish or tray
card (cardboard)
scissors
pieces of thin seaweed (collect as
  many different colours as you can)
paper towels
newspapers

shallow dish

paper towel

*card
(cardboard)*

scissors

seaweed

1 Fill the dish with water. Soak a piece of card (cardboard) in it.

2 Use the scissors to cut off a small piece of seaweed. Float the seaweed on top of the piece of card. Spread out the frond with your fingers by letting it float and fan out into the water.

3 Slowly lift out the card and gently pour off the water. Hold onto the seaweed with your thumb as you pour.

4 Repeat with more weed and drain. Blot with paper towel and leave to dry on the card. If the picture becomes crinkly when it dries, simply soak it again. Press lightly under a pile of newspapers and leave to dry.

Collecting Shells

Sea shells are found and collected on beaches all over the world. You can quickly build up a beautiful collection of shells that will look great displayed in a box or as a picture on the wall.

YOU WILL NEED
bucket
field guide
notebook
pencil
clear varnish
paintbrush
coloured or white card (cardboard)
PVA (white) glue

bucket

clear varnish

PVA (white) glue

card (cardboard)

1 Collect empty, dead shells from the beach into a bucket.

2 Wash them thoroughly in fresh water at home. Leave them outside in the sun to dry for several days. If you do not do this they will become smelly.

3 Use a field guide to identify your shells. Make notes and drawings about them in your nature notebook.

4 Select the best specimen of each shell and paint them with clear varnish.

NATURE NOTE

Some shells are protected and should not be removed from the beach. Be sure to follow local guidelines before taking them.

5 Stick them onto card (cardboard). You can keep the cards with your collection in a box or frame them and hang them on the wall.

Pressed Flowers

Pressing flowers is an excellent way to preserve and keep them. Some specimens in museums are hundreds of years old. You can use pressed flowers to make pictures, or to decorate many different things.

YOU WILL NEED
fresh flowers
tissues or paper towels
flowerpress or book
PVA (white) glue
paper or card (cardboard)

PVA (white) glue

fresh flowers

flowerpress

1 Pick a selection of different flowers.

2 You should not pick wildflowers unless they are weeds growing on private land – and you have the permission of the land-owner.

3 Arrange the flowers on a tissue or a paper towel in a flowerpress or between the pages of a book. If you use a book, make sure that the juice from the flowers will not stain the pages.

4 Spread the petals, and cover them with a second sheet of tissue or paper towel. Replace the top of the flowerpress or close the book. Tighten the bolts on the flowerpress, or, place some more books on top of the book containing the flowers. Leave in a warm, dry place for at least two weeks. Do not peek too soon, or the flowers will not dry properly.

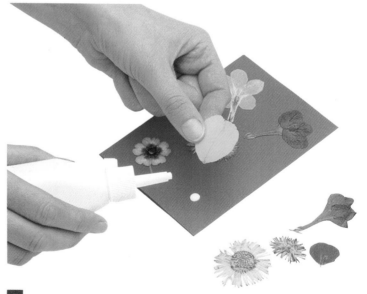

5 When the flowers are dry, carefully lift the dried flowers, and stick them onto paper or card (cardboard) with PVA (white) glue. Use them to decorate greetings cards, writing paper, pictures and lampshades, in fact almost anything you can think of.

Potpourri

Potpourri has been used for centuries to make rooms and stored linen smell nice and fresh.

YOU WILL NEED
fresh flowers
fresh herbs, such as lavender and
    rosemary
scissors
string
foil dish or tray
bowl
spices, such as nutmeg, cinnamon
    sticks and cloves (optional)
airtight jars or bags

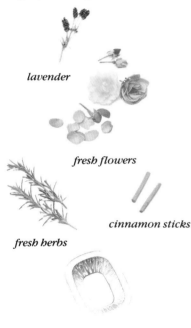

lavender

fresh flowers

cinnamon sticks

fresh herbs

foil dish

string

scissors

1 Pick the flowers and herbs. This plant is lavender.

2 Cut the herbs and tie them into bunches. This plant is rosemary.

3 Hang the bunches of herbs up in a warm place to dry.

4 Put fresh rose petals, small flowers, flower buds, herb leaves and herb flowers onto a foil dish or tray. Put them somewhere warm such as an airing cupboard or near a radiator to dry.

5 When the herbs and flowers are completely dry, strip the leaves from the herb bunches. Put them into a bowl with the dried petals and flowerheads.

6 Add the spices (if using) and mix well. If you wish, you can also add a few drops of perfumed oil. Mix well. Store in airtight jars or bags. To use, place in a shallow dish or basket so that the scent of the flowers, herbs and spices can escape into the air.

Making a Terrarium

Ferns grow in damp places among rocks and in woodlands. You can make yourself an indoor garden by growing them in a large jar or bottle.

YOU WILL NEED
gravel
large plastic jar or bottle with lid or
    stopper
charcoal
potting soil
spoon taped to a long stick
ferns and other plants

plastic jar

plants

spoon taped
to a stick

gravel

charcoal

potting soil

1 Put a layer of gravel in the bottom of the jar or bottle.

2 Put a layer of charcoal on top.

3 Put in a layer of potting soil. Smooth and level the soil with the long-handled spoon.

4 Again using the long-handled spoon, plant the ferns and other plants.

5 Gently add enough water to moisten the soil.

6 Replace the lid or stopper on the jar or bottle. The moisture is kept inside the jar so the plants rarely need watering.

Growing Curly Beans

Here is a simple plant experiment that you can easily do at home.

YOU WILL NEED
paper towels
jam jar
bean or pea seeds such as French (string), runner or mung beans

paper towels

jam jar

bean seeds

1 Fold a piece of paper towel in half, roll it up and put inside the jam jar.

2 Put several bean seeds between the paper and the side of the jam jar. Pour water into the bottom of the jam jar to a depth of approximately 2 cm (¾ in).

NATURE TIP

Bean shoots will always try to grow upwards and towards the light. Look at the large picture on this page. The beans top left are normal beans, growing straight up. The other two jars contain curly beans.

3 When the beans have sprouted a long shoot, turn the jam jar on its side.

4 Put the jam jar on a windowsill and turn the shoot away from the light. Keep turning the jam jar so that the shoot is turned away from the light. You will soon grow curly beans.

Colouring Celery and Flowers

This experiment works almost like magic! You can change white flowers and celery to almost any colour you like.

YOU WILL NEED
jam jar
brightly coloured water-soluble ink or dye
stalk of celery with leaves
white flowers such as carnations, chrysanthemums or daisies

water-soluble ink

celery

flowers

1 Half-fill the jam jar with water.

2 Add some ink or dye.

!NATURE TIP

If you have difficulty making this experiment work, try again with another type or colour of dye. Remember, you will not be able to eat the celery once it has been dyed!

jam jar

3 Stand some celery or flowers in the dye or ink solution.

4 You can make celery or flowers that are half one colour and half another. Split the celery or flower stalk lengthwise and put half in a jam jar of one coloured dye and the other half-stalk in the second jar containing a different colour.

Growing a Pineapple

We all see pineapple in the supermarket. Did you know that you can often use one to grow your own pineapple plant?

YOU WILL NEED
flowerpot
potting soil
fresh pineapple
plastic bag

flowerpot

plastic bag

potting soil

pineapple

1 Fill the flowerpot with potting soil.

2 Twist the top from the pineapple. (You may need an adult to help you with this.)

3 Remove the lower leaves from the stalk. Plant the stalk in the potting soil.

4 Water and place the flowerpot in a plastic bag. Leave in a warm sunny place. Remove the bag when the roots have started to grow. Water your pineapple regularly. Some may eventually produce fruit if kept in a warm greenhouse. Most just make nice houseplants.

Growing Exotic Plants from Seed

Other exotic plants can be grown from the seeds and pips that we find inside fruit.

YOU WILL NEED
fresh fruit
sieve
knife
paper towel
flowerpot
potting soil
plastic bag

paper towel

knife

flowerpot

potting soil

plastic bag

sieve

fresh fruit

! **1** Eat the fruit but save the seeds. Wash the seeds in the sieve. Ask an adult to help you to remove any flesh with a sharp knife. Dry the seeds on a piece of paper towel.

2 Fill the flowerpot with potting soil. Plant the seeds in the soil. Cover them with more potting soil.

3 Water, and put the flowerpot in a plastic bag. Keep in a warm place. Some seeds will sprout quickly, others may take longer. Remove the bag when the sprouts first appear. Keep the flowerpot on a windowsill. Transplant into larger flowerpots as the plants grow larger. The plants in the picture above were grown from supermarket fruit. On the left is a lemon, and on the right a tree tomato.

Autumn Leaves

Every autumn deciduous trees lose their leaves. A tiny layer of cells grow across each leaf stalk like a wall, and the leaf shrivels, dies and falls off. As the leaf dies, it changes colour to yellow, brown, orange, red or purple. Collect fallen leaves and make a collage with them.

YOU WILL NEED
autumn leaves
newspaper
book
large envelope
PVA (white) glue
card (cardboard) or paper

newspaper

book

PVA (white) glue

large envelope

card (cardboard)

autumn leaves

1 Collect as many different autumn leaves as you can.

2 Place the leaves between the folds of a newspaper. Lightly press them by putting a book on top.

3 You can store the flat leaves in an envelope until you need them.

4 Glue the leaves onto a piece of card (cardboard).

5 Make a collection of different types of leaf or use them to make a collage, picture or to decorate greetings cards.

Leafy Jewellery

Use leaves and other natural 'textures' to give pattern and shape to some stunning jewellery. These pieces are very easy to make and are great gifts for your family and friends.

YOU WILL NEED
home oven-bake modelling clay
leaves
blunt knife
pencil (optional)
silver or gold modelling powder
foil dish
varnish
paintbrush
PVA (white) glue
jewellery fittings

foil dish

pencil

modelling clay

knife

jewellery fittings

leaves

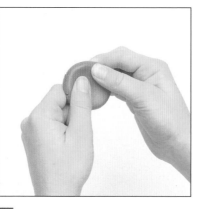

1 Soften the clay between your fingers. Keep pressing it between your fingers until you have made it into a thin sheet.

2 Place the clay on a flat surface. Press a leaf firmly down into the clay.

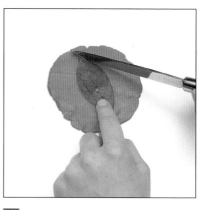

3 Cut the clay around the edge of the leaf with a blunt knife.

4 Lift off the leaf. Then carefully lift up the clay and twist to shape it into a natural leaf shape. Make a hole through the clay with a sharp pencil if you are making a pendant or key ring.

! 5 Dust with silver or gold modelling powder, place on a foil dish or tray, and ask an adult to help you bake the jewellery in an oven according to the clay manufacturer's instructions.

6 Varnish and stick on the jewellery fittings with glue.

Teasel Mice

In days gone by, teasels were used to comb or 'tease' tangled wool before it could be spun. You can use them to make a family of animals.

YOU WILL NEED
teasels
scissors
circle of material 23 cm (9 in) in
    diameter for the body
needle, thread and pins
soft toy stuffing
rectangle of material 23 cm × 10 cm
    (9 in × 4 in) for the arms
rectangle of material 40 cm × 10 cm
    (15 in × 4 in) for the skirt
PVA (white) glue
beads for nose and eyes
fishing line or thread for whiskers
bits and pieces of felt, string, lace
    and ribbon

teasel

soft toy stuffing

PVA (white) glue

material

lace

scissors

1 Collect teasels from hedges and roadsides. Cut the heads from the stalks. Be careful, they are extremely prickly. If you have trouble finding any, teasels are often sold in florists' shops for dried flower arrangements. Alternatively, you can make these mice with pine cones instead.

2 Sew a running stitch around the edge of the circle of cloth for the body. Pull the threads to gather.

3 Put some of the toy stuffing in the middle.

4 Put a teasel on top of the stuffing. Draw the gathering thread in tightly around the base of the teasel. Knot to secure.

5 To make the arms, fold the small rectangle of material in half. Fold in half again. Pin and stitch along its length.

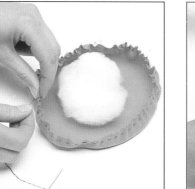

6 Sew a running stitch along one long side of the large rectangle of material for the skirt. Gather. Place around the neck of the teasel and stitch so that the skirt hangs over the body. Put the arms around the neck and stitch them in place above the skirt. Finish by gluing on beads for the eyes and nose, whiskers of fishing line or thread, felt ears and string for the tail. Decorate with ribbon, lace, hats, aprons, cloaks and other clothes. Make a whole family of mice!

Natural Christmas Decorations

In ancient times people in Europe worshipped many different gods of nature. Holly, ivy, mistletoe, yew and other plants held religious meaning for these people. Memories have been passed down with our folklore. Today, these plants are still used to decorate homes at Christmas.

YOU WILL NEED
Christmas greenery
newspaper
dried seed heads
pine cones
gold and silver spray paint
florist's foam for flower arranging
candles
red berries
Christmas tree decorations
ribbon
sticky tape
string
wire
tinsel

spray paint

candle

florist's foam

string

tinsel

1 Gather together some greenery such as holly, ivy, mistletoe, conifer sprigs and other evergreen leaves.

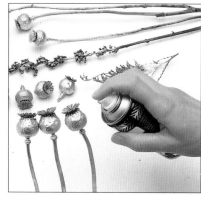

2 Spread out the newspaper in a well ventilated area. Spray dried seed heads and pine cones with gold or silver paint. Allow to dry before using as decorations.

3 To make a table decoration, stick greenery into florists' foam.

4 Push a candle into the middle of the foam. Decorate with sprayed seed heads, cones, berries, Christmas tree decorations and tinsel

5 To make a Christmas wreath, tape or tie greenery around a circle of wire, cane or twigs.

6 Decorate with pine cones and ribbons and other pretty objects. Look at the picture opposite. Can you see some other ideas for natural Christmas decorations?

Cress Eggs

As long as they have water, seeds will grow in many strange places. Have fun growing these cress eggs, you can eat the cress later.

YOU WILL NEED
2 eggs
small bowl
cotton wool (ball)
water
cress seeds
coloured paints
paintbrush

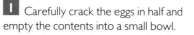

cress seeds

egg

paintbrush

paints

NATURE TIP

Look for other plants growing in unusual places such as on a roof, walls, or rocks.

1 Carefully crack the eggs in half and empty the contents into a small bowl.

2 Moisten a piece of cotton wool (ball) in cold water and place it inside each egg shell half.

3 Sprinkle the cress seeds sparingly onto the cotton wool. Store the egg shells in a dark place for two days, or until the seeds have sprouted, then transfer to a light area such as a windowsill.

4 Paint a jolly face onto each egg shell. Give the egg a haircut and use the 'hair' as a sandwich filling.

Useful Addresses

Many of the organizations below offer junior membership, and information and activities on environmental issues. Others maintain nature reserves open to visitors.

UNITED KINGDOM

British Trust for Conservation Volunteers
36 St Mary's Street
Wallingford
Oxon OX10 0EU
tel: 01865 810 215

(information on practical conservation work)

Countryside and Wildlife Branch
The Environment Service
Calvert House
35 Castle Street
Belfast
BT1 1GU
tel: 01232 314 911

County Naturalist's Trust
Consult your local library for information.

(information about nature reserves in most counties)

English Nature
Northminster House
Northminster Road
Peterborough
Northants PE1 1EU
tel: 01733 349 345

Friends of the Earth
26–28 Underwood Street
London N1 7JO
tel: 0171 490 1555

(information on recycling and other environmental issues)

Greenpeace
Canonbury Villas
London N1 2PN
tel: 0171 354 5100

Royal Society for Nature Conservation
The Green
Witham Park
Waterside South
Lincoln
Lincs LN5 7JR
tel: 01522 544400

(junior membership available)

Royal Society for the Protection of Birds
The Lodge
Sandy
Beds SG19 2DL
tel: 01767 680 551

(organizes Young Ornithologists Club)

Royal Society for the Prevention of Cruelty to Animals
The Manor House
Causeway
Horsham
Sussex RH12 1HG
tel: 01403 264 181

(information on how to help stranded animals)

Worldwide Fund for Nature
Panda House
Weyside Park
Godalming
Surrey GU7 1XR
tel: 01483 426 444

UNITED STATES

American Horticultural Society
7931 East Boulevard Drive
Alexandria, VA 22308
tel: (703) 768 5700

Friends of the Earth
218 D. Street, S.E.
Washington, DC 20003
tel: (202) 783 7400

Friends of the Everglades
101 Westward Drive, #2
Miami Springs, FL 33166
tel: (305) 888 1230

Greenpeace USA
1436 U. St., N.W.
Washington, DC 20009
tel: (202) 462 1177

International Wildlife Conservation
c/o New York Zoological Society
Bronx, NY 10460
tel: (718) 220 5100

Kids for a Clean Environment
P.O. Box 188254
Nashville, TN 37215
tel: (615) 331 7381

National Audubon Society
950 Third Avenue
New York, NY 10022
tel: (212) 979 3000

National Wildlife Federation
1400 16 St., N.W.
Washington, DC 20036
tel: (202) 797 6800

Rainforest Action Network
450 Sansome St., #700
San Francisco, CA 94111
tel: (415) 398 4404

Sierra Club
730 Polk Street
San Francisco, CA 94109
tel: (1415) 776 2211

(ecological association)

Tree People
12601 Mulholland Drive
Beverly Hills, CA 90210
tel: (1818) 753 4600

(tree planting organization)

World Wildlife Fund
1250 24th Street, N.W.
Washington, DC 20037
tel: (1202) 293 4800

Koala Club News
Zoological Society of San Diego
Box 551
San Diego, CA 92112
tel: (619) 231 1515

For local branches, other useful addresses and organizations check your local yellow pages.

AUSTRALIA

Melbourne Zoo Education Service
Elliot Avenue
Parkville, Vic 305
tel: (03) 285 9300

National Parks and Wildlife
See the district office in your local telephone directory. Ask for the Discovery Co-ordinator for activities in your local national park.

Royal Society for the Prevention of Cruelty to Animals
For junior membership, see your local telephone directory for the branch nearest you.

Taronga Zoo Education Centre
Bradleys Head Road
Mosman, NSW 2088
tel: (02) 969 2455

Western Plains Zoo
Education Department
Oblev Road, Dubbo
tel: (068) 82 5888

ACKNOWLEDGEMENTS

The author and publishers would like to thank Emily and Duncan Fitzsimons, Thomas Pickhaver, Edward Gardner and Digby for appearing in the book.